GW00401738

TAKE YOUR EASE & REST AWHILE

ENJOY SOME POETRY

FROM RENVYLE

ALL NEW POEMS OF A CONTEMPORARY NATURE ON
NUMEROUS DIFFERENT SUBJECTS BY AUTHOR & POET

Daniel Sammon

Vol 1

Another book by the same author:

My Great Walk Across Ireland

Front Cover: Daniel Sammon relaxing on 'The White Strand' Renvyle with Mweelrea, Connaught's highest mountain in the background. Also directly behind, across the bay is Croagh Patrick, Ireland's Holy Mountain, which is 'the most climbed mountain' in the entire world.

Back Cover: *The Narrow Little Road*, leading from Tully Village to Gurteen Pier and Tully Beach, Renvyle.

DEDICATION

This book of poems is dedicated
to my grandchildren:
Shane, Jennifer and Holly Heanue
Ardnagreevagh, Renvyle
Amy, Oisin, Dorian & Lydia Sammon
Knocknacarra, Galway
Andrea & Adam Coyne
Mullaghgloss, Renvyle

PROLOGUE

While in the process of writing these poems the first Royal Visit took place of Her Majesty Queen Elizabeth II and the Duke of Edinburgh Prince Philip to the Republic of Ireland in May 2011.

The Visit was an outstanding success from many points of view and many Irish people were enthralled by what the Queen did and said during that Visit.

To mark that momentous occasion and special event in Irish history a number of poems which are contained in this book were composed.

No good in telling a person what you think of them after they've passed away, so in line with that thinking I dispatched just two of those poems to the Royal Couple in London.

Not long afterwards a letter bearing the Royal Stamp of Buckingham Palace arrived through my letterbox.

The anticipation of what it might contain and the excitement in opening that letter was high.

I was informed that Her Majesty and the Duke of Edinburgh were most thankful to me for the lovely poems I had written about their first historic Visit to the Irish Republic, which they enjoyed immensely.

Their letter stated, among other things that the poems were a source of great pleasure and encouragement to them.

It's not everyday I get a letter from Buckingham Palace and it was and is something I very much appreciate.

A few months later in September, just as the Presidential election was beginning to get under way I contemplated on what an outstanding job our current President at the time Mrs Mary McAleese was doing on behalf of our country since taking up office fourteen years previously in 1997.

You guessed it! Another poem on that subject was composed and when I was happy with it, it was dispatched to where? where else but Árus an Uachtarán.

The reply that I received very soon afterwards conveyed to me our President's sincere thanks and appreciation for the poem I composed about: *'The End of President's Term'* as well as two other poems about the Royal Visit which are also included in this book. As a mark of her appreciation, our President also sent me a signed copy of the speech she delivered in Dublin Castle on May 18th 2011 in honour of Her Majesty Queen Elizabeth II.

Needless to say I consider this a great honour also and it is something I am deeply grateful to our President Mrs Mary McAleese for.

Every poet who publishes a compilation of poems especially his first one is understandably a little bit apprehensive about dipping his toe into literary waters and the reaction his writings might receive.

But thanks to the letters I've received from our President Mary McAleese and Her Majesty Queen Elizabeth II in connection with these poems and many other very positive comments about them and my own contentment and satisfaction with lay-out, content and overall production of this book that doesn't apply in my case.

Every poem is or should be a complete story in itself, so if there's one you don't like just go on to the next one! A good poem can be somewhat similarly regarded to a beautiful painting or an attractive lady, not just to be admired or looked at once, but to get its true meaning it should be read a number of times.

Out of the sixty poems contained in this book hopefully there's some to suit everybody's taste.

If you're kind enough to go to the trouble to send your reaction, good or bad, to these poems by email, letter, post or phone, it will be appreciated by me.

Daniel Sammon.

BIRTHDAYS

'Time nor tide waits for no man'
One of my mother's many proverbs

One thing you cannot change or alter in any way is time. It goes on relentlessly and regardless through the centuries and millennia and for that reason among others, man has always been fascinated by it's inexorably hidden mysteries, but he hasn't done a bad job at trying to measure it.

Marking time and dates has always been important to men and indeed women too, maybe even more so.

To mark time has been one of the reasons this book of poetry has come into existence and that is to coincide with the 60th birthday of it's author, which is 13th November.

Some people treat themselves to a little holiday, others throw a bit of a jamboree to celebrate the fact they reached a certain milestone in their lives.

These are excellent things to do but writing a book of poetry and those things are not mutually exclusive.

For all birthday boys and girls especially, I would like to think at least some of these poems will tickle your fancy as you enter into my world of poetry, to where you are very welcome.

For all others, but there are no others because we are all birthday boys and girls at some date on the calendar, whether you have your feet firmly on the ground or travelling one mile high my wish for you is that these poems you will enjoy!

CONTENTS

HEAVEN

As we strolled along by the babbling brook
That's overgrown as in the fairytale book
We were heading for our local beach
Which is very close-by, within our reach

Two little grand-daughters aged nine and eleven
Said 'tell me grandad, where is heaven?'
The sea it was blue and the sky it was clear
I said to them 'tis very nearly, as nice as here'

Try to imagine when you close your eyes
A more beautiful place beyond the skies
With mountains, hillocks and everything so grand
The soft rolling waves and the lie of the land

Then your good health, where you're safe and secure
Every good thing you want, just ask and it's your
Fine schools are awaiting and your whole life ahead
Nice films to watch and good books to be read

But to have all these things is no good at all
If you don't avoid what caused, Man's great downfall
No thanks and no appreciation for all that they've got
Is the reason some people aren't happy with their lot.

MAAM CROSS FAIR

To the Maam Cross Fair he went, to buy a hen
There was no one left, so he went back again
The next time he was told: 'we're sorry, you're out of luck'
'Well if that is the case, then I'll buy a duck'

The duck laid so many fine eggs, to his surprise
He looked much younger, like a man in disguise
His hair turned black again, and his cheeks were rosy
He lived on his own in a cottage, warm and cosy

He thought to himself, as he was only seventy-two
That he might get married, to a woman he hardly knew
He was well aware, he was taking a big chance
But he met her before, at the Bogman's Dance

When he picked up the courage, and asked for her hand
She said if you've road-frontage & cash, that'll be grand
Road-frontage was no problem, but cash he had none
So she put on her coat and away home she did run

Very soon after, the duck she stopped laying
Then to his dismay, his hair started greying
He put on his bicycle clips, fuel in his husqvarna
Bought a new cap and headed for Lisdoonvarna!

Still loads of bachelors around with lots of land that has plenty of road-frontage but Husqvarna motorbikes are a rare sight nowadays!

END OF PRESIDENT'S TERM

As Mary's second term of office, comes to an end
That God's many blessings, He'll continue to send
She served our great Nation with dignity and pride
She's a worthy successor to President Douglas Hyde

She always had her finger, on the pulse of the Nation
In good times and bad, in sorrow or jubilation
She always seemed to do and say the right thing
Everywhere she'd go, joy and happiness she'd bring

She made everybody feel that they were included
The humble and the mighty, no one was excluded
In five hundred years, she'll not be forgotten
From Ardoyne in Belfast to the south of Ballycotten

When the Queen of England came, over on vacation
Together they honoured the heroes of our Nation
The Tricolour fluttered as our National Anthem was sung
The Queen spoke in Gaelic, our own native tongue

Of President Mary McAleese, Ireland can be proud
She carried out her duties without being too loud
As she leaves the Árus, she may shed some silent tears
But she'll have many happy memories of the last 14 years

THE POET

If you're lying on the beach
Or travelling one mile high
You may like a little book
To help the time pass by
It may bring you back in memory
To another time
When life was free and simple
And everything did rhyme

You may be pretty smart, or even know it all
But when you read a verse or two, it's then you will recall
Past forgotten memories, of times from long ago
When as a child you were, at the Connemara Pony Show

In the Brehon times, the poet had high regard
Equal to a bishop and admired as a bard
But for whatever reason, his status did decline
'Twas many years later till his stars again did shine

The beauty of the poem is, that anyone at all
Can put some lines together, if they can even scrawl
You don't have to be a doctor or a student back from Rome
To put coherent thoughts together and compose a lovely poem

In this little book, if some poems you do enjoy
They may bring a longing, or even a teardrop to your eye
Try your hand at writing, one or two yourself
It'll give you satisfaction, your own books on your shelf.

CROAGH PATRICK

The trek up Croagh Patrick is like the journey of life
You could do it on your own but it's better with a wife
At the beginning it may be hard to hold you back
But after climbing for a while the legs get a little slack

The strain and the effort is very worthwhile
You may look exhausted but on your soul there's a smile
You think of your ancestors who walked here before
Without shoes on their feet which must have been sore

At certain parts the slope, gets very steep indeed
Just as in life at times, a little help you might need
You sit down for a rest to give your legs a break
Think of St. Patrick and what he did for our sake

Just after half-way up, the track levels somewhat out
This is merely to prepare you for what's next about
Though the going is quite tough you can't contemplate
Anything but the peak where you can then celebrate

Above at the top you can enjoy a nice picnic
Walk three times around the church and pray for the sick
You thank God for your numerous blessings and riches
And continued protection from An Taisce and witches.

PADDY COYNE'S PUB [1811 - 2011]

On my way home from the bog I called into Paddy Coyne's
Where there's always some craic and Gerard never minds
if the shillings are low and your pockets are skint
If you ask him for a fiver, a tenner will be lent

This very famous pub is, two hundred years old
And in all of those years, it was never once sold
It started selling porter, long before the Famine
And at one stage it also, used to buy and sell salmon

When it was acquired by a man named 'Ould Curley'
It catered for all sorts, the timid and the burly
Not just strong porter and every type of ale
But timber for your roof and slates were for sale

Way back in time, in eighteen hundred and eleven
People thought this place, was a godsend from heaven
If on the White Star Line, you desired to sail
You could get your tickets here, or even call in for your mail

Groceries and everything you wanted for the farm
Gas, coal, briquettes were here to keep you warm
When you passed away they had coffins and drinking sessions
And just across the road there was mass and confessions

We hope it will continue, in spite of all the changes
Though it stopped selling many things, including Stanley ranges
We wish it all the best, for the next two hundred years
And with the famous Celtic thirst, it should have no fears!

PROPERTY AUCTION

At two minutes past six, we left Renvyle coast
Just off the motorway, we stopped for tea and toast
An auction was being held, in the Shelbourne Hotel
It took more than one thousand, the huge hall to fill

On the way in we were, requested for our views
We were told they were desired for the RTE news
The auction got going, at just about eleven
In less than a half hour they had sold six or seven

The properties were selling, just like hot cakes
Apartments and semi d's, all makes and shapes
The selection was interesting, varied and wide
From the docklands in Galway to north of Malahide

Bids were coming over, the internet and phone
From far-off New Zealand and even from Rome
The auction was packed with bidders willing to buy
To show the colour of their money they didn't seem shy

There were properties of all sorts, designs and style
One in particular was located in Renvyle
We thought it a bargain, as 'twas far from a crammer
But it sold in a jiffy, as it came under the hammer.

This auction took place in The Shelbourne Hotel Dublin on 23rd September 2011, at a time when property prices generally were at about 50% of their peak prices (in 2007) and some prices as low as 30% of their peak prices.

FIANNA FAIL 'THINK-IN'

In the depths of the recession the wolf was at the door
But the craic was so good they didn't hear him roar
Enjoying their annual 'think-in' in the Ardilaun Hotel
The food was delicious, you and I were paying the bill

The country was going down the swanny at an alarming rate
They were hoping things would improve, if just left to fate
When you don't drive your own car, or wear your own 'shoes'
Respect for the people can be very easy to lose

With each passing year we were an extra 20 billion in debt
They hadn't a clue how these bills would be met
The EU/ECB/IMF wolf could not understand
Our pensions so generous and our lifestyle so grand

A TD jumped up and shouted *'we'll have another round of beer*
We might well be out of office, this time next year
We have now ruled this country, for so very long
In our bones it just feels, that to us it does belong'

Off the coast we might just find, a well full of oil
And that would then take, the pressure off the boil
The IMF will hardly ever, come and break down the door
For if they do the citizens, with us will wipe the floor.

This 'Think-In' took place in September 2010. Two months later (Nov. 2010) Ireland was obliged to accept an EU/ECB/IMF 'bail-out' and in the process our economic sovereignty went out the window. In the general election in February 2011 Fianna Fail were decimated at the polls.

THE OLD HOMESTEAD

I called to the house as I did when he was there
Looked thro' the window and saw the empty chair
After more than eight decades Da was called home
Now in the old homestead my sister lives alone

In it's heyday it seemed, like the centre of the universe
With the passage of time, everyone there did disperse
Some went across land and some across the foam
Many went to England but none at all went to Rome

In the early sixties the grandparents passed on
We enjoyed happy times there with music and song
As soon as the children, came of age to emigrate
They acquired an old suitcase and were gone out the gate

It's many the time, when the Stations were held
The threshing machine or some trees were being felled
Good neighbours were always, close by at hand
To help with the hay or the bog, or maybe the strand

A large family was reared there, but now it's so quiet
Especially in wintertime on a clear starry night
But it's good someone's still there, to put down the fire
And bring back happy memories of our hearts' desire.

One of many such homesteads around the country!

MONTH OF MAY

On this beautiful morning in the middle of May
The first thing I should do, is to kneel down and pray
To thank God for my numerous blessings and riches
And continued protection from bankers and witches

The fish in the river, the birds in the air
The flowers and the bees and even the hare
They all seem so happy, so joyous and content
To enjoy Mother Nature and all the blessings God sent

At this time of year, it now seems so long ago
Since the dephts of last winter and that heavy snow
Now that's all in the past and the sun it is shining
It is time for the beaches and barbeque dining

Don't put off any longer that picnic you planned
To walk by the shore or climb that mountain so grand
Enjoy every moment while you still have your health
These are your riches, your real source of wealth

To travel to New York in a jet supersonic
Is nothing at all compared to my special tonic
To wake in the morning in the middle of May
And go check in the shed to see did the hen lay

MOTHER

When I was a child at my mother's knee
There was no where else I would rather be
On those happy times I look back and ponder
When my little world was so full of wonder

From a tiny village in the County Clare
She got the Lahinch bus and paid her fare
To Dublin City where she made her way
In the Lucan Spa Hotel she drew her first pay

From Dublin City to Renvyle shore
She travelled west, to go back no more
Settling down with a large family to rear
Kept her busy with little time to spare

Great women like her kept the country going
As the men in the house kept the praties growing
Though times were tough with an economic recession
We were always happy, with no time for depression

Eventually she departed for heaven's shore
Then our hearts were heavy, sad and sore
The memories she left no millionaire could buy
So I hope she's forever happy in the heavenly sky

G A A – LOCAL

There's not many places, where they don't have a club
To get on the local football team, if only as a sub
Is many a young fella's, craving ambition
It's part of our heritage, it's part of our tradition

To wear your club's colours is a great honour
To look back with pride, like the great Matt O'Connor
The hopes of your club as you walk on to the pitch
Resting on your shoulders makes you feel mighty rich

As soon as you score the first couple of points
The team feels so confident, you'd take on even giants
The shouting and cheering that comes from the crowd
You just hear in the background, though they're very loud

You're enjoying it so much, before long there's a break
Soon after half-time, there's a penalty to take
The ref and the players and the crowd go so quiet
As the taker steps up, to put the ball out of sight

Before very long, the final whistle blows
After warm congratulations back home the team goes
Little did the men think, in eighteen eighty four
They would so enrich, Ireland's heritage and folklore

Now in it's 127th year and still going strong! Compare that with many organisations who came, saw, prospered for a while and then vanished!

BÉAL NA mBLÁTH

Beautiful Béal na mBláth
Is the saddest place that I ever saw
When Michael Collins was ambushed and died
Irish women and Irish men cried

Just an ordinary bend on a country road
Because of hatred and bitterness that was sowed
The life of the great Michael Collins was ended
While Irish Freedom he stoutly defended

For many a long year some people mis-understood
His pain and his sacrifice was solely for Ireland's good
Till 2010 when Brian Lenihan gave the Oration
Told the country at large of a hero of our Nation

Now they both enjoy their heavenly reward
As Ministers for Finance they had much in accord
They both did their best for Ireland's prosperity
At home and abroad they used their skill and dexterity

Béal na mBláth is forever a reminder
That hatred and bitterness is a terrible blinder
There's goodness and valour in the hearts of many others
If only we cherish and respect them as brothers

HEADING WEST

At the end of the week I am westward bound
To the fields and the meadows and the corncrake's sound
I leave the city behind for another little while
And drive on homewards to sweet Renvyle

The homemade buttermilk and the corncrake too
If you see them at all, they are very few
The threshing machine and the 'Mac's Smile' blade
Are things of the past, like the turf-cutting spade

It's unrealistic not, to expect new ways
In a constant moving world with each passing phase
We're inclined to hold on, to the things we hold dear
They bring us back in memory to many a long year

When the weekend is over and our batteries are charged
We return to the city so our bank-balance is enlarged
Everyone's in a mad rush and no-one knows why
Unlike the duck in the pond or the clouds in the sky

After many long years in the city, it's nice to retire
In a whitewashed little cottage with an open-fire
Somewhere in the west with the Atlantic for a view
But this is not for everyone, just the lucky few.

THE PRIEST

For decades the people, lived in fear of the priest
If they didn't obey, the power he unleashed
Their souls into hell, would forever be banished
Their bodies were buried and their memories vanished

Their grip was so strong, they thought 'twould last forever
To hold on to power, was their one great endeavour
The weak and the widow, was where they outshone
Because they were over-zealous, their grip is now gone

When the weather was bad and your shoes were worse
If you didn't go to mass, on your head they'd be a curse
It made no difference, if for miles you had to walk
Unless your health wasn't good, you daren't baulk

Among all those priests they were many, genuine and true
Let down by their colleagues, who numbered quite a few
All through many decades, people accepted to be ruled
But sadly now realise, that very often they were fooled

The rules and regulations, that they so loudly preached
Themselves and their colleagues, they so often breached
Especially with young children, who were under their care
While professing their grief and their sorrow to share

Many good Catholics who were not personally affected by the clerical sexual abuse scandals are deeply displeased and hurt by the way those scandals have been handled by the church authorities.

THE NARROW LITTLE ROAD

The narrow little road, winds it's way down to the sea
A secluded sandy beach and exquisite scenery
Just one of Nature's many blessings, if you rest awhile
In north-west Connemara, beautiful Renvyle

St. Patrick's holy mountain, you can see across the bay
Looking back at Renvyle, was where he chose to pray
When his day was done, he sat down and looked out west
He wondered at it's beauty, and wished it forever blest

He didn't have a donkey and cars were not yet invented
So to walk on Renvyle soil, the poor man was prevented
But even so he said, I'll send them my good wishes
And in the seas around them, I'll grant them many fishes

The nature and the landscape, of the place is grand
The mountains and the rivers, the lakes and the land
Everywhere around you, is a pleasure to behold
So relax, enjoy yourself and let your dreams unfold

THE QUEEN'S VISIT

On the 17th of May the Queen of England arrived
To have witnessed this event thank God we survived
The hatchet's long buried and we are now friends again
With our nearest neighbours, some of our own kith and kin

There were many times in the dark distant past
When mistrust and displeasure seemed forever would last
But now that Her Majesty has set foot on Irish soil
Close bonds are established that will last a long while

The two Heads of State are of a similar gender
When one needs a 'bail-out' the other one's a lender
They each serve their country with pride and respect
And from two such fine women it's what you'd expect

From now on Ireland and England will be forever at peace
Except on the sporting field opposition will cease
There's goodwill for each other, the hand of friendship extended
The problems of old and the fences are mended

We welcome the Queen and we welcome her people
To Croke Park in Dublin and Cork's famous steeple
From the west coast of Renvyle to Ballyporeen
From Valentia to Howth and everywhere in between.

As a result of this Royal Visit The Queen and The Royal Family are far more highly regarded now in Ireland and the honour she accorded our patriots was and is very much appreciated!

THAT FAMOUS PINT

They were brought up to the top, to be shown the whole city
When they didn't sample that pint, it seemed such a pity
Prince Philip looked on, but he never put it to his lips
They were hoping he'd grasp it, and take a few sips

The Queen stood there gazing at this marvellous stuff
That 'Paddy' finds so comforting when the going gets rough
Diageo was hoping, that this would boost their sales
And use it 'round the world when telling their tales

The Queen and Prince Philip, weren't going to take a chance
They'd heard how it's inclined, to make you wobble and dance
They enquired where the water, for such fine stuff was acquired
As that pint was left standing there, on the counter to be admired

Just a couple of weeks before, we had the Dalai Lama
And the very next week, we had Barack Obama
On entering the pub, he amazed one and all
By drinking a pint of Guinness, in the town of Moneygall

If Arthur was still living, he would be so very proud
To see his pints of Guinness, were the talk of the crowd
From the Queen to the Prince, and the Prez of the USA
From the shores of Renvyle to dear old Dublin Bay.

IRISH BANKS ON A WINTRY DAY

On a wintry day as he looks out at the rain
He thanks God that between them there is a glass-pane
While the Celtic Tiger was dancing, his mortgage he paid off
So now at the banks he has the good fortune to scoff

Back then they wondered why, more cash he didn't borrow
Had he taken their advice, he would now be full of sorrow
But now that the Government has come to their aid
They blame the plain people, for calling a shovel a spade

Like the circle of Life, everything will come right
In the meantime many people will have gotten a big fright
Then they'll mind their money in a different manner
And into their works they won't throw a spanner

Not too far from now, the sun will be shining
And at it again, some people will be coining
Through hard work and long hours and damn little thanks
They'll pay off their mortgages and to hell with the banks !

This poem and others about the economy were written from the depths of the worst economic recession ever to hit Ireland since the foundation of the State.
What made it so appalling and disastrous was that immediately prior to the onset of the credit-crunch that started in the USA with sub-prime lending and had such a contagious effect was that until then, the Irish economy was booming and officially Ireland was the second richest country in the world! It was easier to believe it than go looking for proof. Unfortunately a lot of people got carried away with that nonsense and will remain paying the price for it for a long time to come.

JAMES CONNOLLY

To take your life so brutally, they strapped you in a chair
For the Cause you loved so dearly, they didn't even care
Inside Kilmainham Jail, in the stone-breakers yard
To break Ireland's will for Freedom, they tried very hard

They didn't know that, with each patriot they shot dead
Every Irish heart they broke, and Irish heart they bled
Strenghtened our determination, to be Sovereign and Free
From the far west of Connemara, to the Irish Sea

James Connolly we will always, remember your sacrifice
Our 1916 Leaders stood tall, while they were only mice
They took you out that ne'er to be forgotten, summer's day
And by firing-squad they shot you dead, on the 12th of May

Together with our other heroes, you all rest in Arbour Hill
You set us an example, by your determination and your will
To hell with their bullets, and to the hell with the foe
Ireland is now Independent, and forever will remain so

Thank you James Connolly, Paddy Pearse and all the others
Those who know our history, will cherish you all like brothers
In a hundred year's time, we'll have vanished without trace
But you'll live on forever, for what you've done for our race

On May 12th 2011 as a tribute to his heroic sacrifice this poem was composed, on his 95th anniversary. We all remember James Connolly but who remembers the names of the soldiers who shot him dead?

POETRY

Whoever it was for, it was not for me
At least that's what I thought, at my mother's knee
Well, maybe not that young but I wasn't tall
When poetry wasn't for me, no, not at all

Whoever they were, they lived way off there
Once it kept them happy, I didn't care
It meant nothing to me, it wasn't my concern
I had enough to do, I didn't want to learn

It was for the arty-farty and people of their ilk
Highly educated or maybe folks who wore silk
As youngsters going to school, we were never taught
The beauty of poetry and the magic that it wrought

It's lovely to hop on a bus, that you almost missed
Or to look into eyes, of a girl you've just kissed
Of all the words, in the English vocabulary
Through poetry you'll best, describe the constabulary

Poetry is for everyone now, for you and for me
cityfolk or country folk, fifteen or ninety-three
It's the way angels converse, one with the other
And lucky are the children, who learn it from their mother

How times and things change!

THE CIVIL WAR

Both sides had the good, of Old Ireland at heart
When the Civil War started, and split the country apart
To make Ireland Free, the price was so high
To settle for something less, they would rather die

The torture and trials, they had to go through
Nowadays they would be endured, by very few
The Brits decided that, they'd pack up and go
All of a sudden our friends became our foe

If only they took stock and stepped back from the brink
Adopted new strategies and had a rethink
Sometimes it's better even when right, to let go
Love for Dear Ireland, there's more than one way to show

Brother fought brother and father fought son
Often the time, it was with a British gun
At the end of it all, distraught and dejected
Peace was restored but only slowly accepted

The Civil War is now, long passed and with hindsight
Forgiveness on both sides is only right
For each was prepared, their own life to give
That Ireland might prosper and her children might live

WAITING AT THE HARBOUR

While sitting at the harbour he waited for his boat to come in
As some came and some left, he sat and he waited again
He always thought of the next one, or maybe the one after that
Being in no rush there was always someone there to chat

He knew that some day his '*pot of gold*' would surely arrive
But when it would come, he was hoping he'd still be alive
Everyone else was coming and claiming their stake
'Twas only a matter of time, from his slumber he would wake

As the years rolled on he wondered why it wasn't coming
Till one summer's day when the honeybees were humming
He noticed a ship that for years was sitting there idle at the quay
All of a sudden he thought, that's the one that's waiting for me

The ship seemed to say: *I've waited so long, where have you been?*
I saw you sitting there but I wasn't sure if it was you, or your twin
When I'm on water, long distance is no trouble to me
But when I reach land you should greet me at the quay

Embarrassed, he got up off his backside and then realised
His life was near over and his whole world almost capsized
The ship he was awaiting, was in the harbour for many a moon
Full of riches and gold that he couldn't get his hands on too soon.

UNBAPTISED CHILDRENS' GRAVEYARD

Walking back through the years on a sandy beach
He counted all the blessings he had within his reach
Though many of his school-friends had gone away far
They'd soon be home again, and with them he'd have a jar

Many moons ago, when as schoolboys young
In the fields they played, as the cuckoo sung
With the sky so clear and the sun always shining
For such idyllic times, our emigrants are pining

The sea is very calm now, and gentle are the waves
Not very far from here, are the little childrens' graves
Many years ago, in the middle of the dark night
Unbaptised babies were buried, without even a light

For decades there they rested, without a mention or a prayer
Except for one old lady, who proved that she did care
For more than half a century, she swore before she died
She'd get them to recognise, the children they denied

Dead children to the local cemetery, the law did not allow
Parents who were not consulted, their heads did meekly bow
That they were unbaptised, was the reason for this law
But that was not sufficient, as Mary Salmon saw.

Well Done, Mary! It may have taken her a long time but on her 80th birthday, through her life-long commitment and perseverance the 'unbaptised childrens' graveyard' at 'Smearoid' at the very edge of the Atlantic Ocean was blessed and consecrated in August 1994.

LEAVING TRALEE

On Monday the second of May I left dear Old Tralee
And arrived back home safe, Sheila, Patricia and me
Some friends I hadn't seen for a long span of time
'Twas lovely to listen to their songs and their rhyme

I knew every spot, I knew every tree
I knew every pub in the town of Tralee
They have a rare talent for *'going with the flow'*
And enjoying the craic wherever they go

Like everywhere else some reach the end of the road
And then they'll depart for their heavenly abode
I visited two cemeteries on Sunday afternoon
And I thought to myself, they're filling-up too soon

In Quane's the *'old characters'* are thin on the ground
But it's great that there's still, some of them around
I visited the place where Robert Emmett rests in peace
After giving his young life trying to end John Bull's lease.

The bank-holiday is over, we're back in Renvyle once more
It's turf-cutting time and the blisters will be sore
The cuckoo has arrived and the swallow's on her tail
'Tis a lovely time in Ireland to travel by foot, bus or rail.

NATASHA & JOSEPHINE

On a Saturday evening as I sit by the fire
I recall many times when it was my heart's desire
To meet up with my cousins who have left Erin's shore
It would be so sad if I saw them no more.

But now that they're back in old Ireland again
Even though it may not be forever amen,
It's good that they're coming, if only for a while
To see all their relations back home in Renvyle.

Very soon their vacation will be at an end
And then they will leave with a very 'God-Send'
They'll bring back with them thoughts and memories galore
Of the happy days and nights they spent on Erin's shore.

When they reach London they'll return to their toil
But always on their mind will be the shores of Renvyle
After they get back, they won't be long there
Till they're planning the next trip and contacting Ryanair.

BRIAN LENIHAN AT BÉAL NA mBLÁTH

There are so many beauty-spots in Ireland
But one for me, will always have a special grah
It's forty three miles west of Cork City
It's name is forever special, beautiful Béal na mBláth

An ambush took place there in August 1922
The men who carried it out, must surely did rue
When Michael Collins' young life was taken away
One of Ireland's greatest misfortunes, to this very day

Though it may have been seen as a dividing point
For decades each side had their own views
'Til the Committee under Dermot Collins
Invited Minister Brian Lenihan for his reviews

A huge crowd gathered for the 88th Commemoration
To hear Brian deliver his wonderful Oration
On that beautiful August Twenty-second, afternoon
Civil-war sentiments ended, not one moment too soon

For many people Collins and Béal na mBláth are the same
But for me memories of Brian Lenihan, will always remain
They were both Ministers for Finance at difficult times
When we now hear their names, we hear heavenly chimes

When Brian and Michael meet on heaven's shore
They'll have many tales to tell about Ireland galore
Their love for their country that they held so dear
It would be so interesting and so lovely to hear !

He did his best for Ireland

AN TAISCE - DESPISED

To think you could set up, a National Organisation
Including mis-fits, and professors of education
They're living well-heeled, in the suburbs of the city
To build one-off houses, oh 'twould be such a pity!

They like to show off, when visitors they entertain
From far overseas, or just from the local terrain
If only for An Taisce, new houses wouldn't blend
Lovely views and our heritage, would come to an end

They don't mind if the attic, the parents will convert
Providing the landscape, new houses don't exert
Living in a caravan, is good enough for you
So long as you don't build a house, blocking the view

Though they live in the city, they will tell you how far
You can go to build your house, and then park your car
They think, they're educated and you don't understand
Our precious heritage, and the lie of the land

If you apply for permission, they will object
They're hoping your application, the Council will reject
If the Council in their wisdom, decide for it to grant
To An Bord Pleanala they'll get straight on to rant

An organisation that's the scourge and nightmare of many a young couple trying to get planning permission in their own local area.

AFTER THE QUEEN'S VISIT

The Royal Visit is over and the Queen has gone home
Close bonds are cemented and deep seeds she has sown
Not just the oak tree, but friendship between our two States
Which will grow and develop at increasing rates

It was enthralling to see, her elegance and style
As she handled each occasion, with dignity and a smile
She won our hearts over, as she spoke in our tongue
She honoured our patriots, as our National Anthem was sung

She is an amazing lady, now we all know it's true
But prior to her Royal Visit, in Ireland it was just a few
Now that she has come over, and enjoyed the four days
It is with respect and affection, we admire her Royal ways

Prince Philip is also, a man to be admired
So tall and so sprightly, much younger men would be inspired
Together they've stolen, the hearts of the Irish people
From Dublin's Fair City, to Cork's famous steeple

Now that they're gone, we feel they're like long-lost relations
Who have come home to visit, from far-off destinations
We hope that because, they've enjoyed their vacation
They'll come back again, for further delectation

FORCED EMIGRATION

As he waved goodbye at the railway station
The tears flowed freely due to forced emigration
He thought he'd left, those days behind
When he had so many of the other kind

For so many years he could hardly keep up
He was going so fast with the Celtic pup
With each new year he got a brand new car
But he always had doubts he was going too far

All of a sudden it came to an abrupt end
Initially he thought it was just a gush of wind
But as things moved on the wind blew colder
The factory closed and he got the cold shoulder

He was used to travelling but only on vacation
'Twas a culture shock, being forced from his Nation
If things ever come right again in this land
Better focus is needed than the last time it was planned

The darkest hour is just before the dawn
His heart is low as he looks out at the lawn
But he won't throw away, his old suitcase and rack
Hopefully he'll need them again soon, for coming back

It's back again like the 1980s and the 1950s all over again! A dreadful indictment on how our economic boom was mismanaged!

MONKS IN LETTERFRACK

To walk in your bare feet in the depths of the ice
On the seashore in Letterfrack wasn't very nice
The monks thought that they, were doing God's bidding
And from our young souls, all sins they were ridding

Letterfrack was a name, that struck terror in our hearts
Picking stones in the land and filling horse-carts
The food you would get at the end of day's toil
'Twould turn your stomach and make you recoil

There was no one to protect us from their reign of terror
With the pain in our faces, just as well there was no mirror
The monks thought that, they could do as they please
And by physical or sexual assault, they would squeeze

The good ones among them, kept their mouths shut
Or into the bad-books, their names would be put
We prayed and worked hard, from morning till night
We were mere children, and they had the might

The monks are now all gone, far from Letterfrack
Pray God that the bastards, will never come back
The village is now quiet, picturesque and serene
At peace with itself, like the monks had never been!

THE POSITIVE SIDE TO NEGATIVITY!

'Thank God' he said when his horse didn't win
'Lucky for me' as he threw his ticket in the bin
But why did he bet at all, if that is so
Why did he waste his time? I'd like to know

Once before when his horse came through
The packet he won, he very soon blew
He lost his licence and almost his life
Spent time on skid-row and seperated from his wife

Now every time when he does the lotto
He says a little prayer that remains his motto
He gets as much satisfaction out of 'almost winning'
There's less temptation and opportunity for sinning

He can still partake and hope that he'll win
Lament his 'near-jackpot' to other men
By not winning he knows, he's far better off
It might drive him to Jameson or maybe Smirnoff

If out of six numbers you might only get five
Thank God for your health, and that you're still alive
If your leg it was broken or you were feeling ill
You couldn't go to the beach or climb the hill!

DIAMOND HILL

In the good old summertime
If a mountain, you'd like to climb
Though it may be, off the beaten track
Make your way to Letterfrack

Start from where, the monks used to be
Once they charged, but now it's free
Park your car and hit the trail
Forget your ESB bill in the mail

As you climb the view gets even better
Over Tullycross and over Letter
Beautiful 'Bofin and majestic Kylemore
Who could ask, for anything more

Across the bay you'll see Mayo
That won the All-Ireland long ago
At the top, you should rest awhile
Enjoy the view of Sweet Renvyle

Be extra careful as you descend
'Cause you don't want, your life to end
When you get back to base again
Go for a pint in the Bard's Den.

Renvyle and Letterfrack have for many decades been a favoured spot for holiday-makers, to find out why pack your bags, come walk among us and enjoy!

HOLLIERS IN RENVYLE

It's the time of year, when the holidays come round
If the health is ok and the cheque-book is sound
The weather is fine but, you don't know where to go
Pack up an old suit-case and head for Ballinasloe

If the fun and the craic there, isn't the best
Continue on travelling, while heading out west
When you pass Galway city, after a while
You'll arrive at a beauty-spot that's called Renvyle

It's mountains and beaches and beautiful views
It's lakes and it's forests and panoramic hues
Have been for decades, a painter's temptation
Where they always find something, for their inspiration

There's craic in the pubs, as you listen to their tales
Of good times and bad, misfortune and wails
No talk you'll find there of economic recession
It's more likely to be, of artistic digression

They'll lament the demise of the threshing machine
And thank God for Our Lady's protection as Queen
The threat to the banning of cutting our bogs
Means you'll now have to, buy more briquettes or logs

CONTENTMENT

I'm just so content to take life easy
To sit back and let the grass grow
If along the way, poetry hadn't found me
I don't know what I'd do or where I'd go

Everything fits into it's own place
Every country and every race
Every corner and every bend
Into one great landscape they all seem to blend

Way-out on the horizon
The ocean and the islands
wild heather and sea breeze
Yours fingers and your shoulder-blades
Your hips and your knees

It's all put there for your enjoyment
But do you spend your time fretting
About the economy and unemployment
Take it easy, go with the flow
Sit back and let the grass grow!

BLONDIE

Though their lives are separated by many miles
He remembers her beautiful face and radiant smiles
The mid-summer sun, high up in the Irish sky
Brings a pain to his heart and a teardrop to his eye

Every day she gets up and gets into her car
Drives to her job even though, it's not very far
It is easy to count, the days that she has missed
Always dependable and there, when she promised

Once in a while, she let's her hair down
But always respectful, she never acts the clown
When she's dolled up and puts on the style
To enjoy her nice company, he'd walk a long mile

After many long years, working in the bank
She was offered promotion and a higher rank
She was tempted and thought about it for a while
But she wouldn't leave home and her local soil

Now she's ready to raise her sail, for a second time
Dreaming of wedding days, and for church-bells to chime
Into strange waters, she's hesitant to dip her toe
So a true-love out there, she may never get to know!

A sad but all too common situation in the modern era!

BIG MORTGAGE

Take these chains from my home and set me free
I never wanted that damn mortgage, it should never be
Where we were did us fine, if we only toe'd the line
But the bug caught us too, and all our friends except a few
Take these chains from my home and set me free

The banks can't pay their bills, and their problems become our ills
The interest that they charge, will very soon be way too large
We can't turn to the State, ask them to wipe clean our slate
When we took on too much debt, that is now to our regret
Take these chains from my home and set me free

If the house went up on fire, though it's far from our desire
The insurance from the claim, though drawn-out and rather lame
Might release us from the hole, when we scored that own-goal
That sunk us deep into such debt, now we're feeling cold and wet
Take these chains from my home and set me free

TIMING IS EVERYTHING

Timing is everything but what do they mean
It's like looking over the balcony, but don't overlean
Like everything else, it's there to be enjoyed
If properly used, the laws of gravity seem defied

When the car-park is packed, what will you do?
Just then a car pulls out and makes room for you
When casting your fishing rod, if you do feel a snatch
Your timing is perfect and you've got a catch

On your wedding day at the altar you wait
For your beautiful bride, who's already 20 minutes late
As you're leaving the church, the bells they are chiming
Proclaiming your good fortune and wonderful timing

When you are born they give you, the time and the date
Not a lot more, except your name and your weight
When golfing it's down to your direction and timing
Your skill and your power, your stroke and your rhyming

At the end of your days, they'll mark where you rest
They'll say nice things about you, like 'he was one of the best'
A big cross they'll put o'er you, that was made out of stone
With your name and address and the year you went home!

HOLY CLOUD ! (OR HOLY COVER-UP)

They thought for a long time, that the Church we'd destroy
By having a few pints and telling the odd lie
Their laws were so strict and their authority so severe
If their rules you neglected 'twould be God help your ear

To miss mass on Sunday was a terrible offence
Because the cow calved was not sufficient defence
The fires of hell blazed and the devil he roared
Promoting evil and danger, that's where he scored

Without the priest in his garb to protect us from harm
Especially young ladies, their guile and their charm
The devil would grab us and hang on to our soul
To be released through confessions we'd pay a heavy toll

The priests were so holy, so correct and so pure
The image they projected was so clean and allure
Young men in their droves lined up to enlist
How little they knew what was covered up in the mist!

Some monks and some nuns, and some priests near and far
Got up to all kinds of tricks in the back of the car
The shock and the horror when this came to our attention
While all of the time 'twas only <u>our</u> sins they'd mention.

Like many other great organisations and powerful empires it could hardly ever be destroyed except from within. Poor Joe Soap feels so badly let down having backed his life on the Catholic Church!

IGOE THE SPY

On your way back to Galway as you travel past Sligo
You may think of a man, whose name it was Igoe
When Collins' Squad had the 'Cairo Gang' wiped out
This fellow appeared and was given 'The Shout'

To be given this job, his neighbours were surprised
And as a result he was forever despised
He knew if he got caught, no mercy he'd be shown
Though he came from Mayo and was considered home-grown

To work for the enemy, he was willing to do
A job he took on, but must surely did rue
The seeds of contempt and hatred he did sow
Meant he never again set foot in Mayo

Lucky for him he didn't get trapped
'Cause Collins' men would have him de-capped
Even the British had more admiration
For the men who were willing, to die for their Nation

Fellows like Igoe are always to be found
Lurking like snails just under the ground
Spying on their neighbours and helping the foe
Just like Judas Iscariot of long long ago.

Michael Collins was the man who had the solution to the problem of spies!

IF ONLY……(THE ECONOMY)

If only just another, million he could make
He'd be so much better off and then a holiday he could take
Life was so short and there was so much money to be made
So many things to do, and so many plans to be laid

If only there was just one, extra day in the week
He could go to the movies or maybe climb 'The Reek'
But everything he did and with every twist and turn
He made so much money, so much he could burn

Then one day he realised, he'd got it all wrong
It just dawned on him suddenly, as he listened to a song
Living to make money was the only 'game in town'
Or so he thought until, the plan badly let him down

When the tide went out, he'd been swimming in the nude
Then in front of all his neighbours he felt a 'right dude'
The bank called in his promissories and asked him to account
His stocks and shares tumbled and his bills began to mount

Even at low prices, he couldn't get a buyer
For his assets and his shares, as his bills mounted higher
Now if he was only back again, to where he started out
But alas he knows too late, he has taken the wrong route

MATURE STUDENT

'Twas always in his head, like a golden rule
That sooner or later he'd go back to school
When he started out first, he couldn't wait to make money
His work was so interesting, lucrative and funny

He discovered quite young what some professors don't realize
As their bank accounts expand and their ego grow in size
It's only when you appreciate, how much you don't know
Your knowledge is pretty limited, that it's liable to grow

Some guys who weren't so smart, took over the reins
Caused economic convulsions and very serious pains
The country went bankrupt and had to be rescued
Their strategies were misguided, their policies skewed

'A little learning is a dangerous thing' we've been told
Add on to that a brass neck and lo and behold!
We live in dodgey times, just trying to keep afloat
On deep choppy waters in a rather small boat

It does make things easier, if education you've got
But that's not sufficient, if it's your only lot
It's far more important, for you to be wise
The whole world you can then, look straight in the eyes.

ARE YOU CRAZY ?

It's a lovely thing to be short of cash
Are you crazy? I can hear you ask
How, and why could that be so?
Can't think of one good reason,
From my head to my toe

It's especially so on a bank-holiday weekend
After a big session, and your head's going round the bend
You may think to yourself, it's a good idea by far
To go to the pub and have yourself another jar

Just then you realise, though your assets are plenty
Your pockets are low and almost empty
The summer is here and the day is sunny
But lo and behold, you have no money

What will you do now? you'll miss the craic!
So you send your wife, to the ATM in Letterfrack
But like British soldiers, when they cross the border
The ATM in Letterfrack is out of order

Now without the craic you'll have to do
But thankfully, times like this are very few
Tomorrow morning your head will be clear
Because you got on fine without those pints of beer

SLAVERY OF TV

You may not realise it but you may be a slave
From soon after you're born 'til you enter the grave
Who then you may ask is my slave-master?
Who is the culprit, that has caused such disaster

From the morn when you wake 'til late in the night
The radio and television try to tell you what's right
Nothing is left to your own intuition
They take over your life from beginning to fruition

The news and the weather is a fine thing indeed
But they'll tell you in elections who will succeed
The wise man will tell them to hell they should go
And get up in the morning when the cock he will crow

Every single day from morning 'til night
If you were foolish, in them you'd delight
Selling their rubbish like the tinkers of old
Although in their midst, there's the odd nugget of gold

It's up to yourself if you want to join in
They don't give a damn, peddling good works or sin
The decision is yours if you want to switch off
Enjoy your own freedom telling them where to scoff

In small doses it is very good, too much of it is bad!

OUR LOSS OF SOVEREIGNTY

As I sit in the pub and wait for my jar
I think of times past when Freedom was afar
People longed for Sovereignty and Independence to come
Little did they think our politicians would be so dumb!

After 800 years the Empire came to an end
The 1916 Rising made it impossible to defend
The War of Independence and the Struggle to be free
Meant Sovereignty became real for you and for me

For 89 years we struggled on, through thick and thin
Then our Leaders thought that greed, was no longer a sin
They lined their pockets and bled the country dry
With mercs and perks and everything under the sky

Too cocky and over-paid, they took their eye off the ball
Derailed the economy and led the country into freefall!
For 800 years people longed to be Sovereign and Free
Now they look back on the short years of Ireland's Sovereignty !

SLEEPING ROUGH

If only they would leave the streets and go on home
Those who are so lucky, to have one of their own
While maybe tomorrow, they can have a ly-in
The garbage truck will soon, be collecting the bin

In a half-hidden doorway, I'm lucky to get forty winks
While rubbish and urine, all around the place stinks
An old lady offered me, a pair of socks for my feet
Most don't even notice me, sleeping here on the street

Some ask if I don't, at all feel the cold
But my story is too long, for them to be told
The temperature is the same, for me as for you
When good luck was dished out, I was in the wrong queue

So I just try to survive, one more night at a time
Some throw me a dirty look, others throw me a dime
I long for the springtime and the early dawn
If I survive to see, the young lambs and the fawn

If the ball had only bounced, round the other way
Like everyone else I could have earned my own pay
Now I tramp the streets, and the lanes of this city
Wishing days into nights, and nights into days, what a pity!

Tough going but a reality!

THE TEACHER

He walked thro' his own village that he passed going to school
Where the teacher beat small children and called them a 'fool'
The energy and effort he put into his vocation
Instilled into the pupils fear and trepidation

If your father was sick or your mother was single
You paid for those 'crimes' as the bamboo cane would tingle
If the sums didn't tot up, or the writing it was wrong
You'd get severe punishment you'd remember so long

The widow, the weak, the poor and the peasant
Their childrens' experience at school wasn't pleasant
Why did those sort of guys ever, contemplate teaching
When they might be better off, maybe at preaching

But the preaching profession, has more than it's share
Of abusing young children, while under their care
Those teachers who were, so horrible and cruel
Were a nightmare for some children who went to their school

Now that is long past, and the rules have now changed
If that happened today, we'd think the teacher was deranged
It was part of the times we lived in, way back then
Hope they're happy in peace, as they're now forgiven

This type of situation was not uncommon in Ireland 50 years ago and more.

MY WALK BACK FROM CLIFDEN

The 2ⁿᵈ half of a 40 kilometre walk from Renvyle to Clifden and back again.

On my return from Clifden as I'm walking back home
I think of our emigrants who were forced to roam
From lovely Mother Ireland that they loved so dear
Even it's name they're enchanted to hear

Tullycross in the distance is a beautiful view
The sea and the mountains have a panoramic hue
The sun it was shining as I passed through Moyard
Where you can go into Acton's for a half pound of lard

The school had a sign saying 'twas still 'Up For Sale'
Where I met Gerry Salmon who was delivering the mail
I continued on my way 'til I got to Letterfrack
Where my legs they were crippled and broken was my back

I still had a few more miles to go
So I didn't sit down or even go slow
I kept on going 'til I reached the 'Angler's Rest'
Where the Guinness they sell is only the best

After a few of pints of Guinness I hit off for the road
And I passed my own cottage where flowers I had sowed
It wasn't far short of the nine o'clock news
When I hung up my walking-stick and took off my shoes.

This Walk was in preparation for 'My Great Walk Across Ireland' which took place in 2009

REFLECTION

When I finished my book, in my mind on reflection
I admired the brave men who initiated the Insurrection
From the chains of bondage they set Old Ireland free
And my wish for the future is, that's how it always should be.

Two little stacks of turf are sitting there so serene
As the mountain caps are white and then the valley turns to green
They're very well protected by their covering of thatch
And it's only in Ireland you will find anything to match.

In centuries past, in a long-distant time
When it was illegal for our church-bells to chime
The people endured pain and tribulation
But always looked forward to the Freedom of their Nation

The Tricolour was hoisted after many long years
That caused many broken hearts and many bitter tears
Not far from now we'll celebrate The Proclamation
And rembember them with pride, thanks and jubilation

THE PRIEST'S ADVICE

From the altar he told them not to receive Holy Communion
If they were living together in an irregular union
In the eyes of the Church they gave bad example
The devil was waiting, their souls for to trample

The preacher seemed unaware, he was wasting his time
For all he was saying, they didn't give a dime
They'd have paid more heed and 'twould be more in his line
To speak of Church scandals as the children were crying

For centuries past on the people, they had an iron grip
If the rules you didn't obey, you'd get a lash of their whip
For most of the flock they were happy to be ruled
But now seem to think, the Church had them fooled

They now carry on as if nothing took place
In spite of the paedophilia and utter disgrace
The people are bombarded with, every other week
To carry on regardless is a terrible cheek

Some people must find the whole thing confusing
If it weren't so serious it be rather amusing
They make stupid laws, to which they cannot attend
Pretending to be super-human and trying to defend.

Moving paedophile priests from one parish to the next only exacerbated the problem instead of solving it!

LIFE IS WHAT YOU MAKE IT

If you're feeling more important than the world thinks you are
Go to the pub and have yourself a jar
If your bank balance is not as big, as you would like it to be
Grab yourself a sun-hat and take a stroll down by the sea

If you're not as suave-looking, as you used to be
Your hair that was once black, is now somewhat differently
Don't worry in the least, take it all in your stride
Life is what you make it, going in and out like the tide

One day you're up, and the next day you're up again
Waiting for the duck to lay and if not, then maybe the hen
The world won't stop turning whatever may befall
It's always been like that for as long as I can recall

The colder the Winter, the greener the Spring
When the flowers start to bud and the birds start to sing
The hotter the summer, the mellower the Fall
As the squirrels make their nest and woodcutters maul

When the world thinks you're as important as you think you are
You've got the balance right, but take it easy on the jar
Don't worry about the bank balance, it'll find it's own level
Even if it doesn't, it can go to the devil.

SWEET RENVYLE

Of all the places, in Old Erin's Isle
There is one spot, called Sweet Renvyle
'Tis where I was born, and reared as a child
Where the praties are sown, and the cabbage is boiled

On summers' evenings, when the sun sinks in the west
Whether fishing or at football, we were forever blest
After cutting the turf, or mowing the hay
We enjoyed a few pints, after lovely fresh tay!

Now that we're far, from the land we were born
We still always think of it night, noon and morn
We long for the day, we'll return there once more
To walk along her mountains, or down by her shore

For tall towers and skyscrapers, I don't give a damn
I'd far more enjoy, seeing a sheep and her lamb
Walking down main streets, it's not easy to reconcile
Longing to be back there, on the slopes of Renvyle

This is the hand of cards, fate gave us to play
And whatever we do, or whatever we say
Though in a foreign land, we will always have a smile
Whenever we think of, the sweet shores of Renvyle.

RENVYLE COTTAGE

There's a cosy little cottage not far from Renvyle shore
If it could only talk it could tell so many tales galore
Built beside the river where the rippling waters flow
It's foundation stones were laid a long long time ago

Long before our grandfathers even went to school
Or the men of 1916 tried to finish British rule
This cottage stood serenely beside the little bridge
It's hedges and it's bushes are a haven for the midge

Two World Wars are only, two of many it has seen
The War of Independence and the Civil in between
The Eurharistic Congress that was held in 1932
Princess Grace's Royal Visit are only just a few

Of sunny summers' evenings it could surely count a lot
With the rays upon the hillocks in this lovely beauty-spot
St. Patrick's holy mountain you can see in the background
While the cuckoo and the honeybees make a lovely sound

From the city way of life, a break you may desire
The constant rush of traffic you at last may start to tire
If in this long established dwelling you would like to stay
Head for Renvyle Cottage, you'll be welcome all the way!

OPEN TURF FIRE

We save the turf to light the fire
We light the fire to boil the kettle
We boil the kettle to make the tea
We make the tea for you and me

When making the tea we put on the pan
On the frying pan we put eggs and bacon
Sausages and pudding, white and black
If you can't polish them off, you must be slack

We pick up the papers and we read the news
They're putting up the price, of cigarettes and booze
The same with petrol, and diesel too
May God forgive them, they haven't a clue

They've no idea how the working man
Is under pressure, from carrying the can
Things are going, from bad to worse
Taking so much money from the public purse

Now the turf they want us, to stop cutting
We were just preparing to do the footing
When he's old and grey it's a man's desire
To smoke his pipe beside an open fire

THE LAST LATE LATE

The Late Late is at an end, at least for the season
But they'll start it up again, if for no other reason
It's going for so long, they won't stop it now
If it was in India they'd call it a sacred cow

Some people have watched it since 40 years ago
And for many it's not, too bad of a show
They may not have much, excitement in their lives
But for others it's worse, than a dose of the hives

With so much hype about it including the host
You would think from watching, all the praise and the boast
The country would collapse and maybe, fall asunder
If a show you missed, there'd be lightening and thunder

Uncle Gaybo himself had a mighty long run
He kept the country entertained with good craic and fun
But in his efforts to stir up, rows and agitation
He upset rural bishops and caused consternation

It will probably go on for another hundred years or so
'Twas there for so long 'twould be a pity to let it go
On it you may see the famous, good and the bad
Some dressed respectfully, and others scantily clad.

It's standing the test of time well!

THE SUMMER IS OVER

The summer is over and long nights are here again
A lovely time of year if you're into paper and pen
To lock up your door and hear the wind whining
Or listen to Margo while your chair is reclining

As your fire is blazing, on the window you hear rain
You might pick up the Bible, to read about Abel and Cain
Or from the tv you might, start planning a cruise
And then later on, watch the nine o'clock news

If you don't think for yourself, RTE will do it for you
But if ever that happens, it's the day you will rue
You won't be able to get up in morn and put on your shoes
Till first you have tuned into, the RTE news

Around your front door, the autumn leaves are blowing
You remember sunny days, when the hay you were mowing
It won't be long now, till the Halloween witches
Will be tramping the roads and crossing the ditches

The days until Christmas, you will soon be counting
Hanging baskets and flower boxes, you'll be dismounting
At this time of year, it's like the Garden of Eden
A time for writing poetry or doing a bit of reading!

THE FINAL HOUR

Death is something you should not fear
When parting with, the ones you love so dear
It affects us all, the entire human race
If it didn't, we'd soon run out of space

When you get, a reasonable spell
The onus is on you, to live it well
Good or bad you're not, gonna last forever
To know that much, you don't have to be clever

At each day's end, you go to sleep
And that does not, give cause to weep
So why should there, be lamentation
When you go on, your final vacation

It is so natural as the day is long
So when my turn comes, I hope I'll be strong
We all accept it, in every other case
Except when we meet it, face to face

To part with loved ones is very sad
But we should thank god, for the good times we've had
You were lucky, if given three or four score
There's many's the one, who got an awful lot lower

WHEN JESUS WAS A LITTLE BOY

When Jesus was a little boy
The stars shone brightly in the sky
Though He was born in a stable
Many years after Cain and Abel

He went to the shop for milk and bread
And at night time, His prayers He said
He always did what He was told
Forever obedient and never bold

As He grew up He had many friends
Loved meeting people, and to their ends
He did His best for all His believers
Healed their blind and cured their fevers

He was only, too well aware
There's always people, who are out there
Just wishing for, a chance to pounce
When told, their evil ways to renounce

There were some who would not accept
What He advised them to reject
To test His word, they said 'if you're boss'
Free yourself from upon the cross.

THE POPE'S ADVICE TO PRIESTS

The poor man's heart was broken
When the awful truth was spoken
The good Polish Pope, Jan Pawel
Who knelt down and kissed the gravel
As a symbol of the love
From Our Father up above

He advised them about the devil
And that he was, full of evil
Roaming round, for any chance
To attack a priest, with his lance
Spurred on by hatred for the world
His wicked schemes, he unfurled

John Paul they thought, was a lovely man
But his good advice didn't fit their plan
Too much wine and not enough prayer
Too close to the ladies was the devil's snare
For some men who choose, to be celibate
Were caught on the hop when it was too late

They're sorry now, his advice was not taken
And so the Catholic Church, is shaken
By men whose lives, they were prepared
To dedicate to the Church, when reared
Pope John Paul now, is happy in heaven
While the devil is planning another 9/11

'MY GREAT WALK ACROSS IRELAND'

When I walked across Ireland in Two Thousand and Nine
I encountered some bad weather but mostly sunshine
The distance was just about two hundred miles long
And while enjoying the walk I sang many a song

I started this feat from my home in Renvyle
Each stretch of the walk was twenty to thirty mile
Through towns and cities and villages I went
Along through the countryside with it's beautiful scent

The struggle for Irish Freedom I was commemorating
Their valour and determination was indeed elating
At the end of it all a Minister met me at the GPO
The scene of The Rising nearly a hundred years ago

The beautiful countryside, the birds and the flowers
Were a joy to behold in this country of ours
When passing through Dublin I visited Arbour Hill
Where the 1916 Leaders are now lying still

To capture these memories I then wrote a book
Concerning this journey that I undertook
It celebrates the long struggle of our dear fatherland
The title of the book is *My Great Walk Across Ireland*